Liverpool Foot

Quiz Book

601 INTERESTING AND ENTERTAINING
QUESTIONS ON LIVERPOOL FC

"My idea was to build Liverpool into a bastion of invincibility. Had Napoleon had that idea he would have conquered the bloody world. My idea was to build Liverpool up and up until eventually everyone would have to submit and give in."

Bill Shankly

This Liverpool Football Club quiz book has been extensively researched and has an incredible 601 questions about Liverpool FC. The questions are all in multiple-choice format and they cover the club's history, honours, records, players, managers, trophies and much more. The questions are sure to test your knowledge of Liverpool FC.

This Liverpool FC Quiz Book is educational, fun and informative and will provide many hours of entertainment for Liverpool fans wherever you live.

Chapter 1: Club Records
(answers on page 61)

1. Who has made the most appearances for the club in total?
    a) Ian Callaghan b) Emlyn Hughes c) Phil Thompson

2. Who is the club's record goal scorer?
    a) Robbie Fowler b) Roger Hunt c) Ian Rush

3. Who has won the most international caps whilst a Liverpool player?
    a) Jamie Carragher b) Ray Clemence c) Steven Gerrard

4. Who has scored the most hat tricks for Liverpool?
    a) Gordon Hodgson b) Roger Hunt c) Ian Rush

5. Who has scored the most penalties for the club?
    a) Steven Gerrard b) Roger Hunt c) Ian St. John

6. Who is the youngest ever goal scorer for the club?
    a) Michael Owen b) Jerome Sinclair c) Raheem Sterling

7. Who is the fastest ever goal scorer for the club?
    a) Jack Balmer b) Robbie Fowler c) Steve McManaman

8. What is the club's record win in any competition?
    a) 9-0 b) 10-0 c) 11-0

9. What is the most number of goals that Liverpool has scored in a league season?
    a) 102 b) 104 c) 106

10. What is the least number of goals that Liverpool has conceded in a league season?
    a) 16 b) 17 c) 18

Chapter 2: Club Related
(answers on page 62)

1. Who was the founder of Liverpool Football Club?
   a) John Houlding b) Michael Holding c) Robert Holding

2. What animal is on the club crest?
   a) Black Bird b) Blue Bird c) Liver Bird

3. Where is the training ground?
   a) Applewood b) Melwood c) Peachwood

4. What is Liverpool's nickname?
   a) The Red Devils b) The Red Roses c) The Reds

5. What is the traditional colour of the away shirt?
   a) Blue b) White c) Yellow

6. Who was the first shirt sponsor?
   a) Candy b) Crown Paints c) Hitachi

7. What is the club's official website?
   a) anfield.com b) liverpool.com c) liverpoolfc.com

8. How much did Gillett and Hicks pay for the club in 2006?
   a) £219 million b) £239 million c) £259 million

9. How much did Fenway Sports Group pay for the club in 2010?
   a) £250 million b) £300 million c) £350 million

10. What is the club's official twitter account?
    a) @lfc b) @liverpool c) @liverpoolfc

Chapter 3: Club History

(answers on page 63)

1. When was Liverpool founded?
    a) 1890 b) 1892 c) 1894

2. What league did they start in?
    a) Lancashire League b) Manchester League c) Merseyside League

3. When did they join the Football League?
    a) 1893 b) 1895 c) 1897

4. Who were Liverpool's first opponents in the Football League?
    a) Corinthians b) Middlesbrough Ironopolis c) Woolwich Arsenal

5. What was the score in their first ever match in the League?
    a) 1-0 b) 2-0 c) 3-0

6. What colour was the club's first kit?
    a) Blue and white b) Green and white c) Red and white

7. When did the club wear all red for the first time?
    a) 1961 b) 1964 c) 1967

8. When was the electronic scoreboards first installed?
    a) 1983 b) 1993 c) 2003

9. How many people died as a result of the Hillsborough disaster in 1989?
    a) 76 b) 86 c) 96

10. How many people died as a result of the Heysel disaster in 1985?
    a) 19 b) 29 c) 39

Chapter 4: Players
(answers on page 64)

1. Who won the UEFA Player of the Year in 2005?
   a) Xabi Alonso b) Steven Gerrard c) Michael Owen

2. Who was known as the 'Flying Pig?
   a) Loris Karius b) Tommy Lawrence c) Simon Mignolet

3. Who was Liverpool's first ever substitute?
   a) Alf Arrowsmith b) Gerry Byrne c) Phil Chisnall

4. Who has made the most Premier League appearances for Liverpool as substitute?
   a) Ryan Babel b) Danny Murphy c) Divock Origi

5. Who designed the prototype for the Adidas Predator football boot?
   a) David Johnson b) Glen Johnson c) Craig Johnston

6. Who is Liverpool's leading Premier League goal scorer?
   a) Robbie Fowler b) Michael Owen c) Luis Suarez

7. Who was the first Liverpool player to lift the FA Cup?
   a) Chris Lawler b) Geoff Strong c) Ron Yeats

8. Who did Steven Gerrard notoriously slip against?
   a) Chelsea b) Crystal Palace c) Manchester City

9. Who is the only Welshman in the Liverpool Hall of Fame?
   a) Ian Rush b) Dean Saunders c) John Toshack

10. Which Liverpool player has the most medals?
    a) Phil Neal b) Graeme Souness c) Phil Thompson

Chapter 5: Managers
(answers on page 65)

1. Who is the club's longest serving manager of all time?
   a) George Kay b) Bill Shankly c) Tom Watson

2. Who is the club's longest serving post war manager?
   a) Bob Paisley b) Bill Shankly c) Don Welsh

3. Who were Liverpool's first managers?
   a) David Ashworth & Tom Werner b) William Barclay & John McKenna c) Matt McQueen & Tom Watson

4. Who was appointed manager in 1896?
   a) George Kay b) George Patterson c) Tom Watson

5. Who was the first Liverpool manager to be sacked?
   a) Phil Taylor b) Roy Evans c) Don Welsh

6. Who was the club's first foreign manager?
   a) Rafa Benitez b) Gerard Houllier c) Jurgen Klopp

7. Who holds a brown belt at judo?
   a) Rafa Benitez b) Roy Evans c) Gerard Houllier

8. Who was the first Liverpool manager to win the LMA Manager of the Year Award?
   a) Brendan Rogers b) Rafa Benitez c) Jurgen Klopp

9. Who has the highest win percentage?
   a) Bob Paisley b) Kenny Dalglish c) Jurgen Klopp

10. Who is the club's most successful manager?
    a) Bob Paisley b) Bill Shankly c) Jurgen Klopp

Chapter 6: Anfield

(answers on page 66)

1. Who was the ground originally the home of before Liverpool's formation in 1892?
    a) Everton b) Stanley Park c) Tranmere

2. Who are the managers honoured with gates at the ground named after them?
    a) Paisley and Souness b) Shankly and Paisley c) Shankly and Souness

3. Which is the largest stand at the ground?
    a) Anfield Road Stand b) The Main Stand c) The Sir Kenny Dalglish Stand

4. Who did Liverpool play against in the record attendance at the ground?
    a) WBA b) West Ham United c) Wolverhampton Wanderers

5. What are the words on the sign leading from the players tunnel to the pitch?
    a) Abandon hope all who enter b) Come on you Reds c) This is Anfield

6. What stands next to 96 Avenue in front of the Main Stand?
    a) Hillsborough Memorial b) John Houlding Memorial c) 96 red balloons

7. What is at the centre of the memorial?
    a) a brass football b) a cross c) an eternal flame

8. Who did England play in the last international at Anfield?
    a) Argentina b) Chile c) Uruguay

9. How long is Liverpool's longest unbeaten run at Anfield?
    a) 75 games b) 80 games c) 85 games

10. What are the words across the Shankly gates?
    a) You are my sunshine b) You to me are everything c) You'll never walk alone

Chapter 7: Club Captains

(answers on page 67)

1. Who was club captain from 1961–1970?
   a) Gerry Byrne b) Gordon Milne c) Ron Yeats

2. Who was club captain from 1973–1979?
   a) Brian Hall b) Emlyn Hughes c) Alec Lindsay

3. Who was club captain from 1979–1981?
   a) Colin Irwin b) Sammy Lee c) Phil Thompson

4. Who was club captain from 1984–1985?
   a) Gary Gillespie b) Phil Neal c) Steve Nicol

5. Who was club captain from 1985-1988?
   a) Alan Hansen b) Steve McMahon c) Nigel Spackman

6. Who was club captain from 1991-1993?
   a) David Burrows b) Ray Houghton c) Mark Wright

7. Who was club captain from 1993-1996?
   a) Mark Kennedy b) Ian Rush c) John Scales

8. Who was club captain from 1997-1999?
   a) Jamie Carragher b) Paul Ince c) Neil Ruddock

9. Who was club captain from 1999-2002?
   a) Markus Babbel b) Jamie Redknapp c) Christian Ziege

10. Who was club captain from 2003-2015?
   a) Xabi Alonso b) Steven Gerrard c) Glen Johnson

Chapter 8: Fans' Player of The Season Award

(answers on page 68)

1. Who won the Fans' Player of the season award for 2019-20?
   a) Trent Alexander-Arnold b) Jordan Henderson c) Sadio Mane

2. Who won the Fans' Player of the season award for 2018-19?
   a) Virgil van Dijk b) Sadio Mane c) Mo Salah

3. Who won the Fans' Player of the season award for 2017-18?
   a) Roberto Firmino b) Sadio Mane c) Mo Salah

4. Who won the Fans' Player of the season award for 2016-17?
   a) James Milner b) Adam Lallana c) Sadio Mane

5. Who won the Fans' Player of the season award for 2015-16?
   a) Emre Can b) Nathaniel Clyne c) Philippe Coutinho

6. Who won the Fans' Player of the season award for 2014-15?
   a) Daniel Agger b) Jamie Carragher c) Philippe Coutinho

7. Who won the Fans' Player of the season award for 2013-14?
   a) Glen Johnson b) Simon Mignolet c) Luis Suarez

8. Who won the Fans' Player of the season award for 2012-13?
   a) Joe Allen b) Steven Gerrard c) Luis Suarez

9. Who won the Fans' Player of the season award for 2011-12?
   a) Daniel Agger b) Martin Skrtel c) Luis Suarez

10. Who won the Fans' Player of the season award for 2010-11?
    a) Dirk Kuyt b) Lucas Leiva c) Pepe Reina

Chapter 9: Shirt Numbers
(answers on page 69)

1. What shirt number is associated with Ian Callaghan?
   a) 8 b) 10 c) 11

2. What shirt number is associated with Tommy Smith?
   a) 4 b) 5 c) 6

3. What shirt number is associated with Jordan Henderson?
   a) 10 b) 11 c) 14

4. What shirt number is associated with Roger Hunt?
   a) 8 b) 10 c) 11

5 What shirt number is associated with Alan Hansen?
   a) 4 b) 5 c) 6

6. What shirt number is associated with Phil Thompson?
   a) 4 b) 5 c) 6

7. What shirt number is associated with Sadio Mane?
   a) 8 b) 9 c) 10

8. What shirt number is associated with James Milner?
   a) 4 b) 7 c) 10

9. What shirt number is associated with Ron Yeats?
   a) 2 b) 5 c) 6

10. What shirt number is associated with John Barnes?
   a) 9 b) 10 c) 11

Chapter 10: Nationalities
(answers on page 70)

1. Where was Bruce Grobbelaar born?
   a) Mozambique b) South Africa c) Zimbabwe

2. Where was Alisson born?
   a) Argentina b) Brazil c) Chile

3. Where was John Arne Riise born?
   a) Denmark b) Norway c) Sweden

4. Where was Sami Hyypia born?
   a) Finland b) Iceland c) Norway

5. Where was Ronnie Whelan born?
   a) Ireland b) Scotland c) Wales

6. Where was Roberto Firmino born?
   a) Brazil b) Chile c) Uruguay

7. Where was Vladimir Smicer born?
   a) Armenia b) Croatia c) Czech Republic

8. Where was Billy Liddell born?
   a) Northern Ireland b) Scotland c) Wales

9. Where was Steve Heighway born?
   a) Indonesia b) Ireland c) Israel

10. Where was Jan Molby born?
    a) Denmark b) Norway c) Sweden

Chapter 11: Bill Shankly

(answers on page 71)

1. Where was Shankly born?
   a) Ireland b) Scotland c) Wales

2. What position did he play?
   a) Centre half b) Left half c) Right half

3. How many times was he capped by Scotland?
   a) 12 b) 22 c) 32

4. Who did he manage before coming to Liverpool?
   a) Grimsby Town b) Hartlepool c) Huddersfield

5. What year did he become manager of Liverpool?
   a) 1956 b) 1959 c) 1961

6. Which trophy was the first he won with Liverpool?
   a) FA Cup b) 2nd Division Championship c) League Cup

7. How many League titles did he win with Liverpool?
   a) 1 b) 2 c) 3

8. Which European trophy did he win during his time as Liverpool manager?
   a) Cup Winners' Cup b) European Cup c) UEFA Cup

9. What was his last game in charge of Liverpool?
   a) FA Cup Final b) League Cup Final c) Charity Shield

10. How many games was he in charge of Liverpool?
    a) 583 b) 683 c) 783

Chapter 12: Bob Paisley
(answers on page 72)

1. Where was Paisley born?
   a) Hethel b) Hethersgill c) Hetton-le-Hole

2. When did he make his debut as a player for Liverpool?
   a) 1946 b) 1947 c) 1948

3. What position did he play?
   a) Centre half b) Left half c) Right half

4. When did he become manager at Liverpool?
   a) 1974 b) 1976 c) 1978

5. How many League titles did he win as manager?
   a) 2 b) 4 c) 6

6. How many League Cups did he win as manager?
   a) 1 b) 2 c) 3

7. How many European Cups did he win as manager?
   a) 2 b) 3 c) 4

8. How many major trophies did he win as manager?
   a) 10 b) 15 c) 20

9. How many Manager of the Year Awards did he win?
   a) 2 b) 4 c) 6

10. How many games was he in charge of Liverpool?
    a) 535 b) 635 c) 735

Chapter 13: Joe Fagan

(answers on page 73)

1. Where was Fagan born?
   a) Leeds b) Leicester c) Liverpool

2. Who did he play over 100 games for?
   a) Bristol City b) Manchester City c) Norwich City

3. What position did he play?
   a) Centre half b) Left half c) Right half

4. When did he join Liverpool?
   a) 1957 b) 1958 c) 1959

5. What was his role under Shankly's management?
   a) Junior team coach b) Physio c) Reserve team coach

6. When did he become manager at Liverpool?
   a) 1981 b) 1983 c) 1985

7. How many League titles did he win as manager?
   a) 0 b) 1 c) 2

8. How many European Cups did he win as manager?
   a) 1 b) 2 c) 3

9. What was his last competitive game as manager?
   a) Charity Shield b) European Cup Final c) League Cup Final

10. How many games was he in charge of Liverpool?
    a) 131 b) 231 c) 331

Chapter 14: Kevin Keegan

(answers on page 74)

1. Where was Keegan born?
   Doncaster b) Lancaster c) Tadcaster

2. Who did Liverpool sign Keegan from?
   a) Newcastle United b) Scunthorpe United c) Southampton

3. Which year was he signed?
   a) 1971 b) 1972 c) 1973

4. What was the transfer fee?
   a) £33,000 b) £55,000 c) £99,000

5. Who did he score against in his debut for Liverpool?
   a) Blackburn Rovers 80 b) Nottingham Forest c) Sheffield Wednesday

6. How many goals did he score for Liverpool?
   a) 80 b) 90 c) 100

7. Who was he sold to?
   a) Bayern Munich b) Juventus c) Hamburg

8. What was the transfer fee?
   a) £500,000 b) £550,000 c) £600,000

9. How many First Division titles did Keegan win at Liverpool?
   a) 1 b) 3 c) 5

10. How many times was he capped for England?
    a) 53 b) 63 c) 73

Chapter 15: Graeme Souness
(answers on page 75)

1. Where was Souness born?
    a) Dundee b) Edinburgh c) Glasgow

2. Who did Liverpool sign Souness from?
    a) Middlesbrough b) Tottenham Hotspur c) Rangers

3. Which year was he signed?
    a) 1978 b) 1978 c) 1979

4. What was the transfer fee?
    a) £250,000 b) £350,000 c) £450,000

5. Who did he take over from as club captain?
    a) Alan Hansen b) Phil Thompson c) Kevin Keegan

6. How many League titles did he win as a player at Liverpool?
    a) 5 b) 6 c) 7

7. Which club did Souness leave Liverpool to continue his playing career?
    a) Bari b) Roma c) Sampdoria

8. Which year was Souness appointed Liverpool manager?
    a) 1991 b) 1992 c) 1993

9. What was the only trophy he won as Liverpool manager?
    a) Charity Shield b) FA Cup c) League Cup

10. How many games was he in charge of Liverpool?
    a) 157 b) 257 c) 357

Chapter 16: Roy Evans
(answers on page 76)

1. Where was Evans born?
   a) Birkenhead b) Bootle c) Skelmersdale

2. When did he make his debut as a player for Liverpool?
   a) 1961 b) 1965 c) 1969

3. What position did he play?
   a) Centre half b) Left half c) Right half

4. How many games did he play for Liverpool?
   a) 9 b) 29 c) 49

5. What was his role at the club under Shankly's management?
   a) Coach b) Kitman c) Physio

6. When did he become Liverpool manager?
   a) 1994 b) 1996 c) 1998

7. Who did he pay a British record fee of £8.5 million for in July 1995?
   a) Nigel Clough b) Stan Collymore c) Paul Ince

8. What was the best position in the League under his management?
   a) 2nd b) 3rd c) 4th

9. What was the only trophy he won as Liverpool manager?
   a) Charity Shield b) FA Cup c) League Cup

10. How many games was he in charge of Liverpool?
    a) 144 b) 244 c) 344

Chapter 17: Gerard Houllier

(answers on page 77)

1. Where was Houllier born?
   a) France b) Italy c) Spain

2. What position did he play?
   a) Defence b) Midfield c) Attack

3. What was the last club he managed before being appointed Liverpool manager?
   a) Lens b) Le Touquet c) Paris Saint-Germain

4. When did he become Liverpool manager?
   a) 1997 b) 1998 c) 1999

5. What was the name often given to the squad he inherited?
   a) Old Boys b) Spice Boys c) Young Boys

6. What three trophies did Liverpool win in 2000-01?
   a) Charity Shield, FA Cup & UEFA Cup b) Charity Shield, League Cup & UEFA Cup c) FA Cup, League Cup & UEFA Cup

7. How many goals did Liverpool score in 2000-01 in all competitions?
   a) 107 b) 117 c) 127

8. What was he rushed to hospital for in 2011?
   a) Cancer b) Heart condition c) Liver Failure

9. What was the best position in the Premier League under his management?
   a) 1st b) 2nd c) 3rd

10. How many games was he in charge of Liverpool?
    a) 207 b) 307 c) 407

Chapter 18: Rafael Benitez
(answers on page 78)

1. Where was Benitez born?
    a) France b) Italy c) Spain

2. What position did he play?
    a) Defence b) Midfield c) Attack

3. What was the last club he managed before being appointed Liverpool manager?
    a) Espanyol b) Valencia c) Villareal

4. When did he become Liverpool manager?
    a) 2002 b) 2003 c) 2004

5. Who was the first player he bought for Liverpool?
    a) Xabi Alonso b) Djibril Cisse c) Josemi

6. Where did Liverpool finish at the end of his first season in charge?
    a) 3rd b) 5th c) 7th

7. What was the best position in the Premier League under his management?
    a) 1st b) 2nd c) 3rd

8. How many trophies did he win at Liverpool?
    a) 2 b) 4 c) 6

9. Who did he win the UEFA Europa League with in 2013?
    a) Chelsea b) Inter Milan c) Napoli

10. How many games was he in charge of Liverpool?
    a) 250 b) 350 c) 450

Chapter 19: Brendan Rodgers

(answers on page 79)

1. Where was Rodgers born?
   a) Northern Ireland b) Scotland c) Wales

2. What position did he play?
   a) Defence b) Midfield c) Attack

3. What was the last club he managed before being appointed Liverpool manager?
   a) Reading b) Swansea City c) Watford

4. When did he become Liverpool manager?
   a) 2010 b) 2011 c) 2012

5. Who was the first player he bought for Liverpool?
   a) Joe Allen b) Fabio Birini c) Daniel Sturridge

6. Where did Liverpool finish at the end of his first season in charge?
   a) 6th b) 7th c) 8th

7. What was the best position in the Premier League under his management?
   a) 2nd b) 3rd c) 4th

8. How many trophies did he win at Liverpool?
   a) 0 b) 1 c) 2

9. How many points did Liverpool finish behind Manchester City in 2013-14?
   a) 2 b) 3 c) 4

10. How many games was he in charge of Liverpool?
    a) 166 b) 266 c) 366

Chapter 20: Jurgen Klopp
(answers on page 80)

1. Where was Klopp born?
   a) France b) Germany c) Italy

2. What is Jurgen Klopp's middle name?
   a) Klipetty b) Manfred c) Norbert

3. What position did he play?
   a) Left Back b) Right Back c) Right Winger

4. What club did he manage before Liverpool?
   a) Bayern Munich b) Borussia Dortmund c) Eintracht Frankfurt

5. When did he become Liverpool manager?
   a) 2014 b) 2015 c) 2016

6. What did he describe himself as at his first press conference?
   a) The arrogant one b) The goofy one c) The normal one

7. What is the tactic he is most known for?
   a) Counter attacking b) Counterfeiting c) Counter pressing

8. Where did Liverpool finish at the end of his first season in charge?
   a) 4th b) 6th c) 8th

9. Who was the first player he bought for Liverpool?
   a) Marko Grujic b) Lorus Karius c) Sadio Mane

10. When did he win his first Premier League Manger of the Season Award?
   a) 2017-18 b) 2018-19 c) 2019-20

Chapter 21: Champions League 2018–19

(answers on page 81)

1. Who did Liverpool finish second to in the group stage?
    a) Napoli b) Paris St. Germain c) Red Star Belgrade

2. Who did Liverpool beat 3-1 on aggregate in the round of 16?
    a) Augsburg c) Bayern Munich c) Werder Bremen

3. Who did Liverpool beat 6-1 on aggregate in the quarter-final?
    a) Benfica b) Porto c) Sporting Lisbon

4. Who did Liverpool beat 4-3 on aggregate in the semi-final?
    a) Barcelona b) Real Madrid c) Seville

5. Where was the final played?
    a) Madrid b) Manchester c) Moscow

6. Who did Liverpool beat in the final?
    a) Juventus b) AC Milan b) Tottenham Hotspur

7. What was the score?
    a) 2-0 b) 2-1 c) 3-1

8. Who scored the first goal?
    a) Divock Origi b) Mo Salah c) Sadio Mane

9. How many of the starting eleven were English?
    a) 1 b) 2 c) 3

10. Who was the captain who lifted the trophy?
    a) Fabinho b) Jordan Henderson c) Georginio Wijnaldum

Chapter 22: Champions League 2004-05

(answers on page 82)

1. Who did Liverpool finish second to in the group stage?
   a) Deportivo La Coruna b) Oympiacos c) Monaco

2. Who did Liverpool beat 6-2 on aggregate in the round of 16?
   a) Bayer Kitzingen b) Bayer Leverkusen c) Bayern Munich

3. Who did Liverpool beat 2-1 on aggregate in the quarter-final?
   a) AC Milan b) Juventus c) Roma

4. Who did Liverpool beat 1-0 on aggregate in the semi-final?
   a) Arsenal b) Chelsea c) Manchester United

5. Where was the final played?
   a) Athens b) Istanbul c) Rome

6. Who did Liverpool beat in the final?
   a) AC Milan b) Juventus c) Roma

7. What was the score after normal time?
   a) 1-1 b) 2-2 c) 3-3

8. What was the score in the penalty shoot out?
   a) 3-1 b) 3-2 c) 4-2

9. Who was the Liverpool goalkeeper in the final?
   a) Scott Carson b) Jerzy Dudek c) Chris Kirkland

10. Who was the captain who lifted the trophy?
    a) Xabi Alonso b) Steven Gerrard c) Sami Hyypia

Chapter 23: European Cup 1983-84
(answers on page 83)

1. Who did Liverpool beat 6-0 on aggregate in the first round?
   a) Odense BK b) Olympiacos c) Omonia

2. Who did Liverpool beat 1-0 on aggregate in the second round?
   a) Athletic Bilbao b) Atletico Levante c) Atletico Madrid

3. Who did Liverpool beat 5-1 on aggregate in the third round?
   a) Benfica b) Porto c) Sporting Lisbon

4. Who did Liverpool beat 3-1 on aggregate in the semi-final?
   a) Dinamo Bucharest b) Dinamo Minsk c) Dinamo Zagreb

5. Where was the final played?
   a) Madrid b) Rome c) Paris

6. Who did Liverpool beat in the final?
   a) AC Milan b) Juventus c) Roma

7. Who scored Liverpool's goal in the 1-1 draw during normal time?
   a) Kenny Dalglish b) Phil Neal c) Ian Rush

8. Who was the Liverpool goalkeeper in the final?
   a) Bob Bolder b) Ray Clemence c) Bruce Grobbelaar

9. Who scored the final winning penalty in the shoot-out?
   a) Phil Neal b) Alan Kennedy c) Ian Rush

10. Who was the captain who lifted the trophy?
    a) Alan Hansen b) Graeme Souness c) Phil Thompson

Chapter 24: European Cup 1980-81

(answers on page 84)

1. Which Finnish team did Liverpool beat 10-1 in the first round, second leg?
     a) ODS b) OPS c) OXS

2. Who did Liverpool beat 5-0 on aggregate in the second round?
     a) Aberdeen b) Celtic c) Rangers

3. Who did Liverpool beat 6-2 on aggregate in the third round?
     a) CSKA Kiev b) CSKA Moscow c) CSKA Sofia

4. Who did Liverpool beat on away goals in the semi-final?
     a) Bayern Munich b) Borussia Dortmund c) Borussia Monchengladbach

5. Where was the final played?
     a) Madrid b) Paris c) Rome

6. Who did Liverpool beat in the final?
     a) Barcelona b) Real Madrid c) Valencia

7. What was the score?
     a) 1-0 b) 2-0 c) 2-1

8. Who scored the winning goal?
     a) Kenny Dalglish b) David Johnson c) Alan Kennedy

9. How many of the starting eleven were English?
     a) 4 b) 6 c) 8

10. Who was the captain who lifted the trophy?
     a) Alan Hansen b) Graeme Souness c) Phil Thompson

Chapter 25: European Cup 1977-78

(answers on page 85)

1. Who did Liverpool beat 6-3 on aggregate in the second round?
    a) Dynamo Dresden b) Dynamo Kiev c) Dynamo Moscow

2. Who did Liverpool beat 6-2 on aggregate in the third round?
    a) Benfica b) Porto c) Sporting Lisbon

3. Who did Liverpool beat 4-2 on aggregate in the semi-final?
    a) Bayern Munich b) Borussia Dortmund c) Borussia Monchengladbach

4. Where was the final played?
    a) Leipzig b) Lisbon c) London

5. Who did Liverpool beat in the final?
    a) Anderlecht b) Brugge b) Standard Liege

6. What was the score?
    a) 1-0 b) 2-0 c) 2-1

7. Who scored the winning goal?
    a) Jimmy Case b) Kenny Dalglish c) David Fairclough

8. How many of the starting eleven were English?
    a) 4 b) 6 c) 8

9. Who was the captain who lifted the trophy?
    a) Alan Hansen b) Emlyn Hughes c) Graeme Souness

10. Who was Liverpool's leading goal scorer in the competition?
    a) Jimmy Case b) Kenny Dalglish c) Ray Kennedy

Chapter 26: European Cup 1976-77

(answers on page 86)

1. Who did Liverpool beat 7 -0 on aggregate in the first round?
   a) Cliftonville b) Crusaders c) Linfield

2. Who did Liverpool beat 3-1 on aggregate in the second round?
   a) Denizlispor b) Izmirspor c) Trabzonspor

3. Who did Liverpool beat 3-2 on aggregate in the third round?
   a) Bordeaux b) Lyon c) St. Etienne

4. Who scored the winning goal in the third round?
   a) David Fairclough b) Ray Kennedy c) Kevin Keegan

5. Who did Liverpool beat 6-1 on aggregate in the semi-final?
   a) FC Basel b) FC Zurich c) Grasshopper Zurich

6. Where was the final played?
   a) Lisbon b) Paris c) Rome

7. Who did Liverpool beat in the final?
   a) Bayern Munich b) Borussia Dortmund c) Borussia Monchengladbach

8. What was the score?
   a) 2-0 b) 3-1 c) 4-2

9. Who scored Liverpool's first goal?
   a) Phil Neal b) Terry McDermott c) Tommy Smith

10. Who scored Liverpool's last goal?
    a) Phil Neal b) Terry McDermott c) Tommy Smith

Chapter 27: UEFA Cup 2001

(answers on page 87)

1. Who did Liverpool beat 1-0 on aggregate in the first round?
   a) Dinamo Bucharest b) Rapid Bucharest c) Steaua Bucharest

2. Who did Liverpool beat 4-2 on aggregate in the second round?
   a) Banik Ostrava b) Slovan Liberic c) Viktoria Plzen

3. Who did Liverpool beat 4-2 on aggregate in the third round?
   a) AEK Athens b) Olympiacos c) Panathinaikos

4. Who did Liverpool beat 2-1 on aggregate in the third round?
   a) Napoli b) Roma c) Udinese

5. Who did Liverpool beat 2-0 on aggregate in the quarter-final?
   a) Benfica b) Porto c) Sporting Lisbon

6. Who did Liverpool beat 1-0 on aggregate in the semi-final?
   a) Barcelona b) Bayern Munich c) Bologna

7. Who did Liverpool beat in the final?
   a) Alaves b) Levante c) Villareal

8. What was the score?
   a) 3-2 b) 4-3 c) 5-4

9. Who scored the winning goal?
   a) Markus Babbel b) Gary McAllister c) own goal by an opponent

10. Who was the captain who lifted the trophy?
    a) Sami Hyypia b) Gary McAllister c) Danny Murphy

(answers on page 88)

1. Who did Liverpool beat 3-2 on aggregate in the first round?
    a) Hamilton b) Hearts c) Hibernian

2. What score did Liverpool beat Real Sociedad on aggregate in the second round?
    a) 5-2 b) 7-2 c) 9-2

3. What score did Liverpool beat Polish side Slask Wroclaw on aggregate in the third round?
    a) 4-1 b) 5-1 c) 6-1

4. Who did Liverpool beat 2-1 on aggregate in the quarter-final?
    a) Dynamo Dresden b) Dynamo Kiev c) Dynamo Tiblisi

5. Who did Liverpool beat 2-1 on aggregate in the semi-final?
    a) Barcelona b) Bayern Munich c) Bologna

6. Who did Liverpool beat in the two-legged final?
    a) Besiktas b) Borussia Dortmund c) Brugge

7. What was the aggregate score?
    a) 3-2 b) 4-3 c) 5-4

8. What was the score at Anfield?
    a) 2-1 b) 3-2 b) 4-3

9. Who was Liverpool's leading scorer in the competition?
    a) Jimmy Case b) Kevin Keegan c) John Toshack

10. Who was the captain who lifted the trophy?
    a) Emlyn Hughes b) Tommy Smith c) Phil Thompson

Chapter 29: UEFA Cup 1973

(answers on page 89)

1. Who did Liverpool beat 2-0 on aggregate in the first round?
    a) Augsburg b) Eintracht Frankfurt c) VfB Stuttgart

2. Who did Liverpool beat -6-1 on aggregate in the second round?
    a) AEK Athens b) Olympiacos c) Panathinaikos

3. What score did Liverpool beat BFC Dynamo (Dynamo Berlin) on aggregate in the third round?
    a) 2-1 b) 3-1 c) 4-1

4. What score did Liverpool beat Dynamo Dresden on aggregate in the third round?
    a) 1-0 b) 2-0 c) 3-0

5. Who did Liverpool beat on the away goals rule in the semi-final?
    a) Arsenal b) Chelsea c) Tottenham Hotspur

6. Who did Liverpool beat in the two legged final?
    a) Bordeaux b) Borussia Monchengladbach c) Braga

7. What was the aggregate score?
    a) 3-2 b) 4-3 c) 5-4

8. What was the score at Anfield?
    a) 3-0 b) 3-1 c) 3-2

9. Who saved a crucial penalty at Anfield?
    a) Ray Clemence b) Frankie Lane c) Grahame Lloyd

10. Who was the captain who lifted the trophy?
    a) Ian Callaghan b) Emlyn Hughes c) Tommy Smith

Chapter 30: Premier League 2019-20
(answers on page 90)

1. How many points did Liverpool finish the season with?
   a) 95 b) 97 c) 99

2. Which team finished second?
   a) Chelsea b) Manchester City c) Manchester United

3. What was the points difference between first and second?
   a) 10 b) 14 c) 18

4. How many goals were scored during the season?
   a) 75 b) 85 c) 95

5. Who was Liverpool's leading goal scorer?
   a) Roberto Firmino b) Sadio Mane c) Mo Salah

6. How many goals did the leading scorer score in the League?
   a) 17 b) 18 c) 19

7. How many games were left when Liverpool won the League?
   a) 5 b) 6 c) 7

8. Who was the first choice goalkeeper during the season?
   a) Adrian b) Alisson c) Kelleher

9. How many players were used in total during the season?
   a) 20 b) 22 c) 24

10. How many League titles have Liverpool now won?
    a) 17 b) 18 c) 19

Chapter 31: First Division 1989-90
(answers on page 91)

1. How many points did Liverpool finish the season with?
   a) 73 b) 76 c) 79

2. Which team finished second?
   a) Arsenal b) Aston Villa c) Tottenham Hotspur

3. What was the points difference between first and second?
   a) 3 b) 6 c) 9

4. How many goals were scored during the season?
   a) 72 b) 75 c) 78

5. Who was Liverpool's leading goal scorer?
   a) John Barnes b) Peter Beardsley c) Ian Rush

6. How many goals did the leading scorer score in the League?
   a) 18 b) 20 c) 22

7. Who did Liverpool beat 9-0 in September 1989 at Anfield?
   a) Charlton b) Coventry City c) Crystal Palace

8. Who was the first choice goalkeeper during the season?
   a) Bruce Grobbelaar b) Mike Hooper c) David James

9. Which midfielder played every game during the season?
   a) Ray Houghton b) Steve McMahon c) Ronnie Whelan

10. How many players were used in total during the season?
    a) 17 b) 19 c) 21

Chapter 32: First Division 1985-86

(answers on page 92)

1. How many points did Liverpool finish the season with?
   a) 80 b) 84 c) 88

2. Which team finished second?
   a) Everton b) Manchester United c) West Ham United

3. What was the points difference between first and second?
   a) 1 b) 2 c) 3

4. How many goals were scored during the season?
   a) 81 b) 85 c) 89

5. Who was Liverpool's leading goal scorer?
   a) Jan Molby b) Ian Rush c) Paul Walsh

6. How many goals did the leading scorer score in the League?
   a) 20 b) 21 c) 22

7. Who did Liverpool beat 6-0 in March 1986?
   a) Newcastle United b) Oxford United c) West Ham United

8. How many clean-sheets did the club keep during the season?
   a) 14 b) 16 c) 18

9. Who did Liverpool beat in the last game of the season to clinch the title?
   a) Arsenal b) Chelsea c) Tottenham Hotspur

10. How many players were used in total during the season?
    a) 16 b) 17 c) 18

Chapter 33: First Division 1979-80

(answers on page 93)

1. How many points did Liverpool finish the season with?
    a) 58 b) 60 c) 62

2. Which team finished second?
    a) Arsenal b) Ipswich Town c) Manchester United

3. What was the points difference between first and second?
    a) 1 b) 2 c) 3

4. How many goals were scored during the season?
    a) 71 b) 81 c) 91

5. Who was Liverpool's leading goal scorer?
    a) Kenny Dalglish b) David Johnson c) Terry McDermott

6. How many goals did the leading scorer score in the League?
    a) 17 b) 19 c) 21

7. Who was the first choice goalkeeper during the season?
    a) Ray Clemence b) Bruce Grobbelaar c) Steve Ogrizovic

8. How many clean-sheets did the club keep during the season?
    a) 10 b) 12 c) 19

9. Who did Liverpool beat in the 1979 Charity Shield pre-season curtain raiser?
    a) Arsenal b) Ipswich Town c) Manchester United

10. How many players were used in total during the season?
    a) 16 b) 17 c) 18

Chapter 34: First Division 1972-73
(answers on page 94)

1. How many points did Liverpool finish the season with?
   a) 58 b) 60 c) 62

2. Which team finished second?
   a) Arsenal b) Ipswich Town c) Leeds United

3. What was the points difference between first and second?
   a) 1 b) 2 c) 3

4. How many goals were scored during the season?
   a) 72 b) 82 c) 92

5. Who was Liverpool's leading goal scorer?
   a) Phil Boersma b) Kevin Keegan c) John Toshack

6. How many goals did the leading scorer score in the League?
   a) 13 b) 15 c) 17

7. Who was the first choice goalkeeper during the season?
   a) Ray Clemence b) Frankie Lane c) Steve Ogrizovic

8. How many clean-sheets did the club keep during the season?
   a) 10 b) 12 c) 14

9. What score did Liverpool beat Manchester United at Anfield?
   a) 1-0 b) 2-0 c) 3-0

10. How many players were used in total during the season?
    a) 16 b) 17 c) 18

Chapter 35: First Division 1963-64

(answers on page 95)

1. How many points did Liverpool finish the season with?
    a) 57 b) 62 c) 67

2. Which team finished second?
    a) Everton b) Manchester United c) Tottenham Hotspur

3. What was the points difference between first and second?
    a) 2 b) 4 c) 6

4. How many goals were scored during the season?
    a) 72 b) 82 c) 92

5. Who was Liverpool's leading goal scorer?
    a) Alf Arrowsmith b) Roger Hunt c) Ian St John

6. How many goals did he score in the League?
    a) 25 b) 28 c) 31

7. How many times did Liverpool score six or more goals in a match?
    a) 2 b) 3 c) 4

8. Who was the first choice goalkeeper during the season?
    a) Jim Furnell b) Tommy Lawrence c) Bert Slater

9. What score did Liverpool beat Manchester United at Anfield?
    a) 1-0 b) 2-0 c) 3-0

10. How many players were used in total during the season?
    a) 17 b) 19 c) 21

Chapter 36: FA Cup 2006

(answers on page 96)

1. Who did Liverpool beat 5-3 away in the third round?
   a) Ipswich Town b) Luton Town c) Northampton Town

2. Who did Liverpool beat 2-1 away in the fourth round?
   a) Bournemouth b) Portsmouth c) Southampton

3. Who did Liverpool beat 1-0 at home in the fifth round?
   a) Manchester United b) Middlesbrough c) Millwall

4. Who did Liverpool beat 7-0 away in the sixth round?
   a) Birmingham City b) Cardiff City c) Stoke City

5. Who did Liverpool beat 2-1 in the semi-final?
   a) Arsenal b) Chelsea c) Manchester United

6. Where was the final played?
   a) Millennium Stadium b) Principality Stadium c) Wembley
   Stadium

7. Who did Liverpool beat in the final?
   a) Manchester United b) Newcastle United c) West Ham United

8. What was the score after normal time?
   a) 1-1 b) 2-2 c) 3-3

9. Who scored in injury time to take the match into extra time?
   a) Djibril Cisse b) Peter Crouch c) Steven Gerrard

10. What was the score in the penalty shoot out?
    a) 3-1 b) 3-2 c) 4-2

Chapter 37: FA Cup 2001
(answers on page 97)

1. Who did Liverpool beat 3-0 at home in the third round?
   a) Leeds United b) Rotherham United c) Scunthorpe United

2. Who did Liverpool beat 2-1 away in the fourth round?
   a) Cambridge United b) Leeds United c) Peterborough United

3. What score did Liverpool beat Manchester City at home in the fifth round?
   a) 4-0 b) 4-1 c) 4-2

4. Who did Liverpool beat 4-2 away in the sixth round?
   a) Blackburn Rovers b) Bristol Rovers c) Tranmere Rovers

5. Who did Liverpool beat 2-1 in the semi-final?
   a) Arsenal b) Tottenham Hotspur c) Wycombe Wanderers

6. Who did Liverpool beat in the final?
   a) Arsenal b) Tottenham Hotspur c) West Ham United

7. What was the score?
   a) 2-1 b) 3-2 c) 4-3

8. Who scored the winning goal?
   a) Stephane Henchoz b) Emile Heskey c) Michael Owen

9. When was the winning goal scored?
   a) 80th minute b) 84th minute c) 88th minute

10. Who was the captain who lifted the trophy?
    a) Steven Gerrard b) Dietmar Hamann c) Sami Hyypia

Chapter 38: FA Cup 1992

(answers on page 98)

1. What score did Liverpool beat Crewe Alexandra away in the third round?
    a) 4-0 b) 4-1 c) 4-2

2. Who did Liverpool need to beat in a replay in the fourth round?
    a) Blackburn Rovers b) Bristol Rovers c) Tranmere Rovers

3. Who did Liverpool need to beat in a replay in the fifth round?
    a) Ipswich Town b) Luton Town c) Northampton Town

4. Who did Liverpool beat 1-0 at home in the sixth round?
    a) Aston Villa b) Birmingham City c) West Bromwich Albion

5. Who did Liverpool beat in the semi-final?
    a) Bournemouth b) Plymouth c) Portsmouth

6. Who did Liverpool beat in the final?
    a) Sheffield Wednesday b) Stoke City c) Sunderland

7. What was the score?
    a) 2-0 b) 3-0 c) 4-0

8. Who scored the first goal?
    a) Ian Rush b) Michael Thomas c) Dean Saunders

9. Who scored the second goal?
    a) Ian Rush b) Michael Thomas c) Dean Saunders

10. Who was the captain who lifted the trophy?
    a) Jan Molby c) Steve Nicol c) Mark Wright

Chapter 39: FA Cup 1986

(answers on page 99)

1. What score did Liverpool beat Norwich City at home in the third round?
   a) 3-0 b) 4-0 c) 5-0

2. Who did Liverpool beat 2-1 away in the fourth round?
   a) Charlton b) Chelsea c) Crystal Palace

3. Who did Liverpool need to beat in a replay in the fifth round?
   a) Birmingham City b) Norwich City c) York City

4. Who did Liverpool need to beat in a replay in the sixth round?
   a) Walsall b) Watford c) Wolverhampton Wanderers

5. Who did Liverpool beat in the semi-final?
   a) Bournemouth b) Portsmouth c) Southampton

6. Who did Liverpool beat in the final?
   a) Everton b) Stoke City c) Sunderland

7. What was the score?
   a) 3-0 b) 3-1 c) 3-2

8. Who scored the first goal for Liverpool?
   a) Craig Johnston b) Kevin MacDonald c) Ian Rush

9. Who was the leading scorer in the FA Cup this season?
   a) Kenny Dalglish b) Ian Rush c) John Wark

10. Who was the captain who lifted the trophy?
    a) Kenny Dalglish b) Alan Hansen c) Jan Molby

Chapter 40: FA Cup 1974
(answers on page 100)

1. Who did Liverpool need to beat in a replay in the third round?
    a) Darlington b) Derby County c) Doncaster Rovers

2. Who did Liverpool need to beat in a replay in the fourth round?
    a) Cambridge United b) Carlisle United c) Colchester United

3. What score did Liverpool beat Ipswich Town at home in the fifth round?
    a) 2-0 b) 4-0 c) 6-0

4. Who did Liverpool beat 1-0 away in the sixth round?
    a) Birmingham City b) Bradford City c) Bristol City

5. Who did Liverpool beat in the semi-final?
    a) Bournemouth b) Leicester City c) Southampton

6. Who did Liverpool beat in the final?
    a) Arsenal b) Newcastle United c) Watford

7. What was the score?
    a) 3-0 b) 3-1 c) 3-2

8. Who scored the first goal for Liverpool?
    a) Steve Heighway b) Kevin Keegan c) Alec Lindsay

9. Who was the leading scorer in the FA Cup this season?
    a) Steve Heighway b) Kevin Keegan b) John Toshack

10. Who was the captain who lifted the trophy?
    a) Peter Cormack b) Brian Hall c) Emlyn Hughes

Chapter 41: Steven Gerrard
(answers on page 101)

1. Where was Gerrard born?
    a) Middlesex b) Midlothian c) Merseyside

2. How old was he when he joined the Liverpool Academy?
    a) 9 b) 10 c) 11

3. How old was he when he made his first team debut?
    a) 17 b) 18 c) 19

4. How old was he when he was made captain?
    a) 23 b) 24 c) 25

5. How many appearance did he make in total for the club?
    a) 510 b) 610 c) 710

6. How many times did Gerrard captain Liverpool?
    a) 413 b) 443 c) 473

7. How many times did he win Liverpool Player of The Season award?
    a) 2 b) 3 c) 4

8. Which club did he move to after Liverpool?
    a) DC United b) LA Galaxy c) New York Red Bulls

9. How many England caps did he win?
    a) 94 b) 104 c) 114

10. What is the first team he managed?
    a) Aberdeen b) Celtic c) Rangers

Chapter 42: Emlyn Hughes

(answers on page 102)

1. Where was Hughes born?
   a) Alnwick b) Barrow-in-Furness c) Carlisle

2. How old was he when he died?
   a) 57 b) 67 c) 77

3. Which club did Liverpool buy him from?
   a) Barrow b) Blackburn c) Blackpool

4. What transfer fee did Liverpool pay for him?
   a) £45,000 b) £65,000 c) £85,000

5. What was his nickname?
   a) Clumsy Wumsy b) Crazy Horse c) Pork Chop

6. How many First Division titles did he win with Liverpool?
   a) 2 b) 4 c) 6

7. Which club did he move to after Liverpool?
   a) Hull City c) Rotherham United c) Wolverhampton Wanderers

8. How many England caps did he win?
   a) 42 b) 52 c) 62

9. What team did he manage?
   a) Rotherham United b) Sheffield Wednesday c) Sheffield United

10. What TV program did Hughes appear as a team captain for a number of years?
   a) Question of Sport b) QI c) Question Time c) They think it's all over

Chapter 43: Jordan Henderson

(answers on page 103)

1. Where was Henderson born?
   a) Southampton b) Stoke c) Sunderland

2. How tall is he?
   a) 5 feet 11 inches b) 6 feet c) 6 feet 1 inch

3. Which club did Liverpool buy him from?
   a) Middlesbrough b) Newcastle United c) Sunderland

4. What transfer fee did Liverpool pay for him?
   a) £16 million b) £26 million c) £36 million

5. Who did he play against on his Liverpool debut?
   a) Southampton b) Stoke City c) Sunderland

6. Who did he reject a move to in August 2012?
   a) Crystal Palace b) Fulham c) West Ham United

7. When did he captain Liverpool for the first time?
   a) September 2014 b) October 2014 c) November 2014

8. When did he win the Football Writers Association Footballer of the Year Award?
   a) 2017/18 b) 2018/19 c) 2019/20

9. What position does he normally play?
   a) Defence b) Midfield c) Attack

10. What shirt number does he wear?
    a) 12 b) 13 c) 14

Chapter 44: Ian Rush

(answers on page 104)

1. Where was Rush born?
   a) Ireland b) Scotland c) Wales

2. Which club did Liverpool buy him from?
   a) Chester City b) Chesterfield c) Huddersfield

3. What transfer fee did Liverpool pay for him?
   a) £300,000 b) £400,000 c) £500,000

4. What was his nickname?
   a) The Assassin b) The Boss c) The Ghost

5. How many First Division titles did he win with Liverpool?
   a) 3 b) 4 c) 5

6. How many goals did he score for Liverpool?
   a) 229 b) 287 c) 346

7. Which year did he win FWA Footballer of the Year Award?
   a) 1982 b) 1983 c) 1984

8. Which club did he move to after Liverpool?
   a) AC Milan b) Juventus c) Roma

9. How many international caps did he win?
   a) 53 b) 73 c) 93

10. What team did he manage?
    a) Chester City b) Chesterfield c) Huddersfield

Chapter 45: Mo Salah

(answers on page 105)

1. Where was Salah born?
   a) Algeria b) Egypt c) Libya

2. Which club did Liverpool buy him from?
   a) Chelsea b) Fiorentina c) Roma

3. What transfer fee did Liverpool pay for him?
   a) £26.9 million b) £36.9 million c) £46.9 million

4. Who did he score against on his Liverpool debut?
   a) Watford b) West Ham United c) Wolverhampton Wanderers

5. What is his religion?
   a) Christian b) Hindu c) Muslim

6. How many goals did he score in the Premier League in the 2017/18 season?
   a) 28 b) 30 c) 32

7. When did he win the PFA Players' Player of the Year Award?
   a) 2017/18 b) 2018/19 c) 2019/20

8. When did he win the Football Writers Association Footballer of the Year Award?
   a) 2017/18 b) 2018/19 c) 2019/20

9. How many goals did he score in his first 100 Premier League appearances?
   a) 50 b) 60 c) 70

10. What is his nickname?
    a) The Bearded Maradona b) The Muslim Messi c) The Pharaoh

(answers on page 106)

1. Where was Owen born?
   a) Chichester b) Chester c) Rochester

2. What was his nickname?
   a) Midget Gem b) Midget Man c) Midget Mike

3. How old was he when he made his first team debut?
   a) 17 b) 18 c) 19

4. How many appearances did he make in total for the club?
   a) 197 b) 297 c) 397

5. How many goals did he score in total for the club?
   a) 118 b) 138 c) 158

6. Which club did he move to after Liverpool?
   a) Newcastle United b) Manchester United c) Real Madrid

7. How much was the transfer fee?
   a) £8million b) £18million c) £28million

8. How many international caps did he win?
   a) 79 b) 89 c) 99

9. How many goals did he score for England?
   a) 20 b) 30 c) 40

10. When did he win European Footballer of the Year?
    a) 2000 b) 2001 c) 2002

Chapter 47: Robbie Fowler

(answers on page 107)

1. Where was Fowler born?
   a) Leicester b) Leeds c) Liverpool

2. What was his nickname?
   a) God b) Jesus c) The Main Man

3. How old was he when he made his first team debut?
   a) 17 b) 18 c) 19

4. How many appearances did he make in total for the club?
   a) 339 b) 369 c) 399

5. How many goals did he score in total for the club?
   a) 143 b) 163 c) 183

6. Which club did he move to after he left Liverpool the first time?
   a) Cardiff City b) Leeds United c) Manchester City

7. How much was the transfer fee?
   a) £10million b) £12million c) £14million

8. How many international caps did he win?
   a) 26 b) 36 c) 46

9. How many goals did he score for England?
   a) 7 b) 17 c) 27

10. Where was his first managerial appointment?
    a) Australia b) Bangladesh c) Thailand

Chapter 48: Jamie Carragher
(answers on page 108)

1. Where was Carragher born?
   a) Birkenhead b) Bootle c) Burtonwood

2. Who did he support when he was a youngster?
   a) Arsenal b) Everton c) Sunderland

3. How tall is he?
   a) 5 feet 11 inches b) 6 feet 1 inch c) 6 feet 3 inches

4. How old was he when he made his first team debut?
   a) 17 b) 18 c) 19

5. How many appearances did he make in total for the club?
   a) 707 b) 737 c) 767

6. How many League appearances did he make in total for the club?
   a) 508 b) 548 c) 588

7. How many international caps did he win?
   a) 28 b) 38 c) 48

8. How many trophies did he win at the club?
   a) 7 b) 9 c) 11

9. Which TV channel did he join as a pundit after leaving the club?
   a) BT Sport b) Sky Sports c) ITV Sport

10. What was the title of his autobiography?
    a) Carra b) Jamie C. c) Utility Man

Chapter 49: Virgil van Dijk
(answers on page 109)

1. Where was van Dijk born?
    a) Belgium b) France c) The Netherlands

2. Which club did Liverpool buy him from?
    a) Bournemouth b) Portsmouth c) Southampton

3. What transfer fee did Liverpool pay for him?
    a) £55 million b) £65 million c) £75 million

4. What position does he normally play?
    a) Right back b) Centre half c) Left back

5. Who did he score against on his debut?
    a) Burnley b) Everton c) Fulham

6. What is his nickname?
    a) The Boss b) The Dyke c) The Dude

7. What name is on the back of his shirt?
    a) van Dijk b) Virgil c) VVD

8. Which Scottish club did he play for between 2013 and 2015?
    a) Aberdeen b) Celtic c) Motherwell

9. Which season did he win PFA Player of the Year Award?
    a) 2017-18 b) 2018-19 c) 2019-20

10. Which season did he win UEFA Player of the Year Award?
    a) 2017-18 b) 2018-19 c) 2019-20

Chapter 50: More Nationalities

(answers on page 110)

1. Where was Lucas Leiva born?
   a) Argentina b) Brazil c) Paraguay

2. Where was Jerzy Dudek born?
   a) Albania b) Poland c) Ukraine

3. Where was Philippe Coutinho born?
   a) Argentina b) Brazil c) Chile

4. Where was Martin Skrtel born?
   a) Serbia b) Slovakia c) Slovenia

5. Where was Javier Mascherano born?
   a) Argentina b) Brazil c) Chile

6. Where was Alan Hansen born?
   a) Northern Ireland b) Scotland c) Wales

7. Where was Luis Suarez born?
   a) Argentina b) Chile c) Uruguay

8. Where was Georginio Wijnaldum born?
   a) Belgium b) Luxembourg c) The Netherlands

9. Where was Dietmar Hamann born?
   a) Austria b) Germany c) Hungary

10. Where was Sadio Mane born?
    a) Ivory Coast b) Mali c) Senegal

Chapter 51: More Shirt Numbers

(answers on page 111)

1. What shirt number is associated with Kenny Dalglish?
   a) 7 b) 8 c) 9

2. What shirt number is associated with Emlyn Hughes?
   a) 4 b) 5 c) 6

3. What shirt number is associated with Mo Salah?
   a) 10 b) 11 c) 14

4. What shirt number is associated with Ian Rush?
   a) 9 b) 10 c) 11

5 What shirt number is associated with Virgil van Dijk?
   a) 4 b) 5 c) 6

6. What shirt number is associated with Steven Gerrard?
   a) 4 b) 8 c) 11

7. What shirt number is associated with Kevin Keegan?
   a) 7 b) 8 c) 9

8. What shirt number is associated with Jamie Carragher?
   a) 21 b) 23 c) 25

9. What shirt number is associated with Graeme Souness?
   a) 4 b) 8 c) 11

10. What shirt number is associated with Robbie Fowler?
    a) 9 b) 10 c) 11

Chapter 52: 1960s Transfers
(answers on page 112)

1. Which club was Ian St. John signed from in 1961?
   a) Hearts b) Motherwell c) Partick Thistle

2. Which club was Ron Yeats signed from in 1961?
   a) Dundee b) Dundee United c) Hibernian

3. Which club was Peter Thompson signed from in 1963?
   a) Bolton Wanderers b) Preston North End c) Tranmere Rovers

4. Which club was Ray Clemence signed from in 1967?
   a) Norwich City b) Scunthorpe United c) Tottenham Hotspur

5. Which club was Tony Hateley signed from in 1967?
   a) Arsenal b) Chelsea c) West Ham United

6. Which club was Tony Hateley sold to in 1968?
   a) Aston Villa b) Chelsea c) Coventry City

7. Which club was Alun Evans signed from in 1968?
   a) West Bromwich Albion b) West Ham United c) Wolverhampton Wanderers

8. Which club was Alec Lindsay signed from in 1969?
   a) Blackburn Rovers b) Bolton Wanderers c) Bury

9. Which club was Larry Lloyd signed from in 1969?
   a) Blackburn Rovers b) Bristol City c) Bristol Rovers

10. Which club was Roger Hunt sold to in 1969?
    a) Blackburn Rovers b) Bolton Wanderers c) Bury

Chapter 53: 1970s Transfers
(answers on page 113)

1. Which club was John Toshack signed from in 1970?
   a) Cardiff City b) Swansea City c) Wrexham

2. Which club was Tommy Lawrence sold to in 1971?
   a) Doncaster Rovers b) Raith Rovers c) Tranmere Rovers

3. Who did the club sign from non-league club South Liverpool in 1973?
   a) Jimmy Case b) Steve Heighway c) Joey Jones

4. Which club was Terry McDermott bought from in 1974?
   a) Bury b) Newcastle United c) Nottingham Forest

5. Which club was Ray Kennedy bought from in 1974?
   a) Arsenal b) Charlton Athletic c) Crystal Palace

6. Which club was Phil Neal bought from in 1974?
   a) Newcastle United b) Northampton Town c) Nottingham Forest

7. Which club was Joey Jones bought from in 1975?
   a) Cardiff City b) Swansea City c) Wrexham

8. Which club was Alan Kennedy bought from in 1978?
   a) Newcastle United b) Middlesbrough c) Sunderland

9. Which club was Ronnie Whelan bought from in 1979?
   a) Finn Harps b) Home Farm c) Sligo Rovers

10. Which club was Bruce Grobbelaar bought from in 1979?
    a) Montreal Impact c) Toronto c) Vancouver Whitecaps

Chapter 54: 1980s Transfers
(answers on page 114)

1. Which club was Steve Nicol bought from in 1981?
    a) Aberdeen b) Arbroath c) Ayr United

2. What was the transfer fee paid to Brighton for Mark Lawrenson in 1981?
    a) £500,000 b) £700,000 c) £900,000

3. Who did Liverpool pay Middlesbrough £650,000 for in 1981?
    a) Phil Boersma b) Craig Johnston b) Graeme Souness

4. Which club did David Johnson and Kevin Sheedy leave Liverpool for in 1982?
    a) Aston Villa b) Everton c) Leicester City

5. Who was the first signing made by Bob Paisley in May 1983?
    a) Jim Beglin b) Gary Gillespie c) Michael Robinson

6. Which club was Jan Molby bought from in 1984?
    a) Ajax b) Eindhoven c) Feyenoord

7. Which club was John Wark bought from in 1984?
    a) Ipswich Town b) Norwich City c) Middlesbrough

8. Who was the first signing made by Kenny Dalglish in September 1985?
    a) Gary Ablett b) Steve McMahon c) Barry Venison

9. Who was sold to Queens Park Rangers in July 1986 and who later came back to the club in a coaching capacity?
    a) Steven Caulker b) Sammy Lee c) Nigel Spackman

10. Which club was John Aldridge bought from in 1987?
    a) Colchester United b) Oxford United c) Peterborough United

Chapter 55: 1990s Transfers

(answers on page 115)

1. Which club was Jamie Redknapp bought from in 1991?
   a) Bournemouth b) Southampton c) Tottenham Hotspur

2. Which club was Mark Wright bought from in 1991?
   a) Derby County b) Oxford United c) Southampton

3. Who joined Liverpool in 1991, just two years after scoring a late goal for Arsenal against Liverpool at Anfield in a crucial title decider?
   a) Jimmy Carter b) Michael Thomas c) Alex Oxlade-Chamberlain

4. Which club was David James bought from in 1992?
   a) Aston Villa b) Portsmouth c) Watford

5. Which club was Stan Collymore bought from in 1992?
   a) Aston Villa b) Newcastle United c) Nottingham Forest

6. Who did Liverpool pay Tottenham £2.5 million for in 1993?
   a) Nathan Ruddock b) Neil Ruddock c) Nigel Ruddock

7. Which club was Patrik Berger bought from in 1996?
   a) Borussia Dortmund b) Red Star Belgrade c) Slavia Prague

8. Which club was Danny Murphy bought from in 1997?
   a) Charlton Athletic b) Crewe Alexandra c) Crystal Palace

9. What was the transfer fee paid to Newcastle United for Dietmar Hamann in 1999?
   a) £7 million b) £8 million c) £9 million

10. Which club was Vladimir Smicer bought from in 1999?
    a) Bordeaux b) Lens c) Slavia Prague

(answers on page 116)

1. Which club was Emile Heskey bought from in 2000?
   a) Birmingham City b) Leicester City c) Wigan Athletic

2. Which club was Gary McAllister bought from in 2000?
   a) Coventry City b) Leeds United c) Leicester City

3. Which club was Jerzy Dudek bought from in 2001?
   a) Ajax b) Eindhoven c) Feyenoord

4. Which club was John Arne Riise bought from in 2001?
   a) Fulham b) Monaco c) Roma

5. Which club was Harry Kewell bought from in 2003?
   a) Leeds United b) Manchester United c) Sheffield United

6. Which club was Xabi Alonso bought from in 2004?
   a) Real Betis b) Real Madrid c) Real Sociedad

7. Who did Liverpool pay Barcelona £6 million for in 2004?
   a) Josemi b) Luis Garcia b) Fernando Morientes

8. Which club was Pepe Reina bought from in 2005?
   a) Barcelona b) Valencia c) Villareal

9. Which club was Dirk Kuyt bought from in 2006?
   a) Fenerbache b) Feyenoord c) Fiorentina

10. Which club was Martin Skrtel bought from in 2008?
    a) Rostov b) Rubin Kazan c) Zenit St Petersburg

Chapter 57: 2010-2020 Transfers
(answers on page 117)

1. Which club was Andy Carroll bought from in 2011?
   a) Manchester United b) Newcastle United c) West Ham United

2. Which club was Luis Suarez bought from in 2011?
   a) Ajax b) Feyenoord c) Groningen

3. Which club was Fernando Torres sold to in 2011?
   a) Atletico Madrid b) Chelsea c) AC Milan

4. Which club did Liverpool sign Philippe Coutinho from in 2013?
   a) Espanyol b) Inter Milan c) PSG

5. Which club did Liverpool sign Adam Lallana from in 2014?
   a) Bournemouth b) Portsmouth c) Southampton

6. Which club did Liverpool sign Roberto Firmino from in 2014?
   a) 1860 Munich b) 1899 Hoffenheim c) Hannover 96

7. Which club did Liverpool sign James Milner from in 2015?
   a) Aston Villa b) Leeds United c) Manchester City

8. Which club did Liverpool sign Sadio Mane from in 2016?
   a) Metz b) Red Bull Salzburg c) Southampton

9. Which club did Liverpool sign Alex Oxlade-Chamberlain from in 2017?
   a) Arsenal b) Southampton c) Tottenham Hotspur

10. Which club did Liverpool sign Mohamed Salah from in 2017?
    a) Chelsea b) Fiorentina c) Roma

Chapter 58: Who said that?
(answers on page 118)

1. Some people believe football is a matter of life and death. I am very disappointed with that attitude. I can assure you it is much, much more important than that.
   a) Benitez b) Paisley c) Shankly

2. Nothing had changed in my routine, except that when I went down the chippy and got me special fried rice, it would be wrapped in a newspaper that had my picture all over it.
   a) Collymore b) Fowler c) Owen

3. They compare McManaman to Heighway and he's nothing like him, but I can see why - it's because he's a bit different.
   a) Keegan b) Rush c) Souness

4. If you're in the penalty area and don't know what to do with the ball, put it in the net and we'll discuss the options later.
   a) Benitez b) Paisley c) Shankly

5. What can you do playing against eleven goalposts?
   a) Benitez b) Rodgers c) Shankly

6. I've been here during the bad times too - one year we came second.
   a) Houllier b) Klopp c) Paisley

7. That's a question mark everyone's asking.
   a) Grobbelaar b) McAteer c) Whelan

8. That would've been a goal had it gone inside the post.
   a) Collymore b) Heskey c) Owen

9. The difference between Everton and the Queen Mary is that Everton carry more passengers.
   a) Evans b) Moran c) Shankly

10. You can't say my team aren't winners. They've proved that by finishing fourth, third and second in the past three seasons.
    a) Benitez b) Houllier c) Rodgers

Chapter 59: Who said that too?

(answers on page 119)

1. If a player is not interfering with play or seeking to gain an advantage, then he should be.
    a) Benitez b) Paisley c) Shankly

2 It's a huge honour to wear the number 7 shirt. I think about the legends Dalglish, Keegan and that Australian guy.
    a) McManaman b) Milner c) Suarez

3. If Everton were playing at the bottom of my garden, I'd shut the curtains.
    a) Evans b) Moran c) Shankly

4. I don't think there is anyone better, that is the reality of how I see it.
    a) Benitez b) Evans c) Rodgers

5. We had the best two teams in Merseyside; Liverpool and Liverpool reserves.
    a) Moran b) Paisley c) Shankly

6. I always used to put my right boot on first, and then obviously my right sock.
    a) Neal b) Nicol c) Venison

7. When I've got nothing better to do, I look down the league table to see how Everton are getting along.
    a) Benitez b) Evans c) Shankly

8. Liverpool is full of the kind of people who go out on Monday and couldn't care less about Tuesday morning.
    a) Hamann b) Hyypia c) Molby

9. It was like playing in a foreign country.
    a) Keegan b) Rush c) Souness

10. I want to build a team that's invincible, so that they have to send a team from bloody Mars to beat us.
    a) Benitez b) Klopp c) Shankly

Chapter 60: Sir Kenny Dalglish

(answers on page 120)

1. Where was Kenny Dalglish born?
   a) Aberdeen b) Dundee c) Glasgow

2. Who did Liverpool sign Dalglish from?
   a) Celtic b) Clydebank c) Cowdenbeath

3. Which year was he signed?
   a) 1975 b) 1976 c) 1977

4. What was the transfer fee?
   a) £330,000 b) £440,000 c) £550,000

5. When did he become player manager?
   a) 1984 b) 1985 c) 1986

6. How many goals did he score for Liverpool?
   a) 118 b) 145 c) 172

7. How many times did he win the Football Writers Association Player of the Year Award?
   a) 1 b) 2 c) 3

8. How many First Division titles did he win as a player and manager in total?
   a) 6 b) 7 c) 8

9. How many times was he capped for Scotland?
   a) 82 b) 92 c) 102

10. When was he knighted?
    a) 2017 b) 2018 c) 2019

Chapter 1: Club Records – Answers
(questions on page 1)

1. Ian Callaghan.
2. Ian Rush.
3. Steven Gerrard. He won 114 caps for England.
4. Gordon Hodgson.
5. Steven Gerrard.
6. Michael Owen.
7. Jack Balmer.
8. 11-0.
9. 106.
10. 16.

Chapter 2: Club Related - Answers
(questions on page 2)

1. John Houlding.
2. Liver Bird.
3. Melwood.
4. The Reds.
5. White.
6. Hitachi.
7. liverpoolfc.com
8. £219 million.
9. £300 million.
10. @lfc.

Chapter 3: Club History - Answers
(questions on page 3)

1. 15th March 1892.
2. Lancashire League.
3. 1893.
4. The club's first match in the Football League was against Middlesbrough Ironopolis.
5. 2-0.
6. Blue and white.
7. November 25th 1964 was the first time Liverpool wore a kit entirely in red.
8. 2003.
9. 96.
10. 39.

1. Steven Gerrard.
2. Tommy Lawrence.
3. Phil Chisnall.
4. Ryan Babel.
5. Craig Johnston.
6. Robbie Fowler.
7. Ron Yeats.
8. Chelsea.
9. Ian Rush.
10. Phil Neal is the most decorated player in Liverpool history with 22 Winners medals. In fact no Englishman can boast more medals.

Chapter 5: Managers – Answers
(questions on page 5)

1. The club's longest serving manager in time was Tom Watson who managed for 19 years from 1896 to 1915. The longest serving manager by matches was Bill Shankly who was in charge for 783 games, whilst Watson was in charge for 742 games.
2. Bill Shankly.
3. William Barclay and John McKenna.
4. Tom Watson.
5. Don Welsh.
6. Gerard Houllier.
7. Rafa Benitez.
8. Brendan Rodgers.
9. Sir Kenny just shades it from Jurgen Klopp (stats prior to 2020/21 season). Dalglish won 60.91% of his 307 games in charge.
10. Bob Paisley.

Chapter 6: Anfield - Answers

(questions on page 6)

1. Everton.
2. Bill Shankly and Bob Paisley.
3. The Main Stand is the largest stand at the ground.
4. The record attendance was when 61,905 people attended an FA Cup tie against Wolverhampton Wanderers in February 1952.
5. This is Anfield.
6. The Hillsborough Memorial.
7. An eternal flame.
8. England beat Uruguay 2-1 in the last international played at Anfield – in March 2006.
9. The longest unbeaten run at home was from January 1978 to January 1981 and was for an incredible total of 85 games. I reckon this will be beaten in 2020 though.
10. You'll never walk alone.

66

Chapter 7: Club Captains - Answers

(questions on page 7)

1. Ron Yeats.
2. Emlyn Hughes.
3. Phil Thompson.
4. Phil Neal.
5. Alan Hansen.
6. Mark Wright.
7. Ian Rush.
8. Paul Ince.
9. Jamie Redknapp.
10. Steven Gerrard.

Chapter 8: Player of the Season Award – Answers
(questions on page 8)

1. Jordan Henderson.
2. Virgil van Dijk.
3. Mo Salah.
4. Sadio Mane.
5. Philippe Coutinho.
6. Philippe Coutinho.
7. Luis Suarez.
8. Luis Suarez.
9. Martin Skrtel.
10. Lucas Leiva.

Chapter 9: Shirt Numbers - Answers

(questions on page 9)

1. Callaghan – 11.
2. Smith – 4.
3. Henderson – 14.
4. Hunt -10.
5. Hansen – 6.
6. Thompson – 4.
7. Mane – 10.
8. Milner – 7.
9. Yeats – 5.
10. Barnes – 10.

Chapter 10: Nationalities - Answers

(questions on page 10)

1. Bruce Grobbelaar was born in South Africa, but Bruce being Bruce, he represented Zimbabwe at international level.
2. Alisson was born in Brazil.
3. John Arne Riise was born in Norway.
4. Sami Hyypia was born in Finland.
5. Ronnie Whelan was born in Ireland.
6. Roberto Firmino was born in Brazil.
7. Vladimir Smicer was born in the Czech Republic.
8. Billy Liddell was born in Scotland.
9. Steve Heighway was born in Ireland.
10. Jan Molby was born in Denmark.

Chapter 11: Bill Shankly - Answers
(questions on page 11)

1. Scotland.
2. Right half. It's almost the equivalent of a holding midfielder in modern football.
3. Shankly played 12 times for Scotland from 1938 to 1943, in five full and seven wartime internationals.
4. Huddersfield.
5. Shankly became manager of Liverpool on 14th December 1959.
6. The Second Division championship in 1961-62.
7. 3 League Titles.
8. The UEFA Cup which was won in 1973 by beating Borussia Mönchengladbach 3-2 on aggregate.
9. Shankly's last competitive game in charge of the club was the 1974 FA Cup Final when Liverpool beat Newcastle United 3-0 at Wembley.
10. Shankly was manager of Liverpool for 783 games from 1959 until his retirement in 1974.

Chapter 12: Bob Paisley - Answers

(questions on page 12)

1. He was born in Hetton-le-Hole in County Durham on 23rd January 1919.
2. He made his debut in 1946.
3. He played left half which is similar to a holding midfielder in modern football.
4. 1974.
5. Six.
6. Three.
7. Three.
8. He won 20 major trophies at the club: - 6 League Titles, 3 League Cups, 6 Fa Charity Shields, 3 European Cups, 1 UEFA Cup and 1 UEFA Super Cup, and is the most successful manager in Liverpool's history.
9. He won the Manager of the Year Award a record six times.
10. Paisley was manager of Liverpool for 535 games from 1974 until his retirement in 1983.

Chapter 13: Joe Fagan – Answers
(questions on page 13)

1. He was born in Walton, Liverpool.
2. He played 158 games for Manchester City.
3. He played right half.
4. He joined Liverpool as part of the coaching staff in 1958.
5. When Shankly was appointed in December 1959, he made Fagan reserve team coach.
6. He was appointed manager of Liverpool on 1st July 1983.
7. One.
8. One.
9. His last game was the European Cup Final against Juventus on 29th May 1985.
10. Fagan was manager of Liverpool for 131 games from July 1983 until his retirement on 29th May 1985 directly after the Heysel Stadium disaster.

Chapter 14: Kevin Keegan - Answers
(questions on page 14)

1. Keegan was born in Doncaster in South Yorkshire.
2. Scunthorpe United.
3. 1971.
4. £33,000.
5. On 14th August 1971, Keegan made his Liverpool debut at Anfield against Nottingham Forest, scoring after just 12 minutes.
6. Keegan scored exactly100 goals in 323 appearances for Liverpool.
7. Hamburg SV.
8. £500,000.
9. Keegan won three League Titles at Liverpool – 1972-73, 1975-76 and 1976-77.
10. Keegan was capped 63 times by England.

Chapter 15: Graeme Souness - Answers

(questions on page 15)

1. Edinburgh.
2. Middlesbrough.
3. 10th January 1978.
4. £350,000.
5. Phil Thompson.
6. Five.
7. Sampdoria.
8. 1991.
9. FA Cup – in 1992.
10. Souness was manager of Liverpool for 157 games from April 1991 until January 1994.

(questions on page 16)

1. **1.** Bootle.
2. **2.** 1965.
3. **3.** Centre half.
4. **4.** 9.
5. **5.** Coach.
6. **6.** January 1994.
7. **7.** Stan Collymore.
8. **8.** 3rd.
9. **9.** League Cup - in 1995.
10. **10.** Evans was manager of Liverpool for 144 games from April 1991 until November 1998.

Chapter 17: Gerard Houllier - Answers
(questions on page 17)

1. France.
2. Midfield.
3. Paris Saint-Germain.
4. 1998.
5. In 1999, Houllier began started to rebuild re-build the team, and restore discipline to a squad that had been labelled widely as 'Spice Boys'.
6. League Cup, FA Cup and the UEFA Cup.
7. 127 goals in total – 72 in the League, 17 in the FA Cup 18 in the League Cup, and 19 in the UEFA Cup.
8. Heart condition.
9. 2nd.
10. Houllier was manager of Liverpool for 307 games from July 1998 to May 2004.

Chapter 18: Rafa Benitez - Answers

(questions on page 18)

1. Spain.
2. Defence.
3. Valencia.
4. 2004.
5. Djibril Cisse who cost Liverpool £14.5 million in July 2004.
6. 5th.
7. 2nd.
8. Four - Champions League 2005 and EUFA Super Cup 2005, Community Shield 2006 and FA Cup 2006.
9. Chelsea.
10. Benitez was manager of Liverpool for 350 games from June 2004 to June 2010.

Chapter 19: Brendan Rodgers - Answers
(questions on page 19)

1. Rodgers was born in Northern Ireland.
2. Defence.
3. Swansea City.
4. 2012.
5. Fabio Borini who cost Liverpool £10.5 million in July 2012.
6. 7th.
7. 2nd.
8. 0.
9. Despite being five points clear with three games to go in April 2014, Liverpool slipped up by losing 2-0 at home to Chelsea, and drawing 3-3 at Crystal Palace, despite being 3-0 up, to finish the season second, just two points behind Manchester City.
10. Rodgers was manager of Liverpool for 166 games from June 2012 to October 2015.

Chapter 20: Jurgen Klopp - Answers
(questions on page 20)

1. Stuttgart, Germany.
2. Norbert.
3. Right back.
4. Borussia Dortmund.
5. 8th October 2015.
6. He said he was 'the normal one'.
7. Klopp is a proponent of Gegenpressing, a counter pressing tactic in which the team, after losing possession of the ball, immediately attempts to win back possession, rather than falling back to regroup.
8. 8th.
9. Marko Grujic was the first player Klopp bought for Liverpool joining from Red Star Belgrade in January 2016 for £5.1 million.
10. 2019-20.

Chapter 21: Champions League 2018–19 Answers
(questions on page 21)

1. Paris St. Germain.
2. Bayern Munich.
3. Porto.
4. Barcelona. After losing the away leg 0-3, Liverpool won the return leg 4-0 in a memorable match under floodlights at Anfield.
5. The final was played at the Metropolitano Stadium in Madrid.
6. Tottenham Hotspur.
7. 2-0.
8. Mo Salah scored with a penalty in the second minute of the game.
9. Two Englishmen started the match for Liverpool; Trent Alexander-Arnold and Jordan Henderson.
10. Jordan Henderson.

1. Monaco won the group. Liverpool came second in the group on goal difference pipping Olympiacos mainly thanks to a late Steven Gerrard goal in the 3-1 home victory.
2. Bayer Leverkusen.
3. Juventus.
4. Chelsea were beaten 1-0 on aggregate, thanks to a disputed goal at Anfield from Luis Garcia.
5. Istanbul was the setting for Liverpool's fifth win of the European Cup / Champions League.
6. AC Milan.
7. 3-3. Who could ever forget the most remarkable comeback after being 0-3 down at half time.
8. 3-2.
9. Jerzy Dudek.
10. Steven Gerrard. Boy did he deserve to lift the trophy after his performance during the match, and the season for that matter.

Chapter 23: European Cup 1983-84 – Answers
(questions on page 23)

1. Odense.
2. Athletic Bilbao.
3. Benfica.
4. Dinamo Bucuresti.
5. Rome.
6. Roma.
7. Phil Neal.
8. Bruce Grobbelaar. He is fondly remembered during the shoot out for wobbling his legs to distract the Italian striker Graziani who promptly blazed the ball over the bar.
9. Alan Kennedy. Liverpool won the penalty shoot-out 4-2.
10. Graeme Souness.

Chapter 24: European Cup 1980-81 - Answers
(questions on page 24)

1. Finnish side Oulun Palloseura, commonly known as OPS.
2. Aberdeen.
3. CSKA Sofia. CSKA is an abbreviation for Central Army Sports Club.
4. Bayern Munich. The first match at Anfield ended 0-0 and the return leg in Munich finished 1-1.
5. Paris.
6. Real Madrid.
7. 1-0
8. Alan Kennedy.
9. Of the eleven players who started the match for Liverpool, eight were English and three were Scottish. All five subs were English.
10. Phil Thompson.

Chapter 25: European Cup 1977-78 – Answers
(questions on page 25)

1. Dynamo Dresden.
2. Benfica.
3. Borussia Monchengladbach.
4. Wembley Stadium, London.
5. FC Brugge.
6. 1-0.
7. Kenny Dalglish.
8. Of the 11 players who started the match for Liverpool, 8 were English and 3 were Scottish. How times have changed.
9. Emlyn Hughes.
10. Jimmy Case was the leading goal scorer during the competition with four goals in total.

1. Crusaders.
2. Trabzonspor.
3. Saint-Etienne.
4. Supersub David Fairclough scored the winning goal in the 84th minute. Until he scored, St. Etienne were going through on the away goals rule.
5. FC Zurich.
6. The Olympic Stadium, Rome.
7. Borussia Monchengladbach.
8. 3-1.
9. Terry McDermott.
10. A Phil Neal penalty secured a deserved victory in the 82nd minute.

Chapter 27: UEFA Cup 2001 – Answers
(questions on page 27)

1. Rapid Bucharest.
2. Slovan Liberic.
3. Olympiacos.
4. Roma.
5. Porto.
6. Barcelona.
7. Alaves.
8. 5-4.
9. In the 115th minute a Spanish defender scored into his own goal to give Liverpool the 'golden goal' to enable the club to win the UEFA Cup for the third time in the club's history.
10. Sami Hyypia.

Chapter 28: UEFA Cup 1976 – Answers

(questions on page 28)

1. Hibernian.
2. 9-2.
3. 5-1.
4. Dynamo Dresden.
5. Barcelona.
6. Club Brugge.
7. 4-3.
8. 3-2.
9. Jimmy Case, who scored 5 goals during the competition.
10. Emlyn Hughes.

Chapter 29: UEFA Cup 1973 – Answers
(questions on page 29)

1. Eintracht Frankfurt.
2. AEK Athens.
3. 3-1.
4. 3-0.
5. Tottenham Hotspur.
6. Borussia Monchengladbach.
7. 3-2
8. 3-0.
9. Ray Clemence.
10. Tommy Smith.

Chapter 30: Premier League 2019-20 – Answers

(questions on page 30)

1. 99 points, which is a club record.
2. Manchester City.
3. 18.
4. 85.
5. Mo Salah.
6. 19.
7. Liverpool clinched the title with a League record 7 games to spare.
8. Alisson.
9. 24.
10. 19.

Chapter 31: First Division 1989- 90 - Answers
(questions on page 31)

1. 79 points.
2. Aston Villa.
3. 9 points.
4. 78.
5. John Barnes.
6. 22.
7. Crystal Palace.
8. 21.
9. Steve McMahon.
10. 21.

1. 88 points.
2. Everton.
3. 2 points.
4. 89.
5. Ian Rush.
6. 22.
7. Oxford United were thrashed 6-0 at Anfield. Just four weeks later Oxford United won the League Cup.
8. 16. Incredibly 8 of those clean-sheets came in the last nine games.
9. Liverpool won the title at Stamford Bridge after beating Chelsea 1-0 with Kenny Dalglish scoring the goal.
10. 18.

Chapter 33: First Division 1979-80 - Answers

(questions on page 33)

1. 60 points. This was in the days of two points for a win.
2. Manchester United.
3. 2.
4. 81.
5. David Johnson.
6. 21.
7. Ray Clemence.
8. 19.
9. Arsenal were beaten in the 1979 Charity Shield.
10. 17 players were used during the season.

Chapter 34: First Division 1972-73 - Answers
(questions on page 34)

1. 62 points. This was in the days of two points for a win..
2. Arsenal.
3. 3 points.
4. 72.
5. Kevin Keegan and John Toshack were actually joint leading goal-scorers for the season.
6. Keegan and Toshack scored 13 goals each in the League.
7. Ray Clemence.
8. 14.
9. 2-0.
10. Just 16 players were used throughout the whole 42 game season.

Chapter 35: First Division 1963-64 – Answers
(questions on page 35)

1. 57 points. This was in the days of two points for a win..
2. Manchester United.
3. 4 points.
4. 92.
5. Roger Hunt.
6. 31.
7. 4.
8. Tommy Lawrence.
9. 3-0.
10. 17.

Chapter 36: FA Cup 2006 – Answers

(questions on page 36)

1. Luton Town.
2. Portsmouth.
3. Manchester United.
4. Birmingham City.
5. Chelsea.
6. Millennium Stadium, Cardiff.
7. West Ham United.
8. 3-3.
9. Steven Gerrard.
10. 3-1.

(questions on page 37)

1. Rotherham United.
2. Leeds United.
3. 4-2.
4. Tranmere Rovers.
5. Wycombe Wanderers.
6. Arsenal.
7. 2-1.
8. Michael Owen. He scored both of Liverpool's goals.
9. The winner came with a beautiful left foot strike in the 88th minute.
10. Sami Hyypia.

1. 4-0.
2. Bristol Rovers were beaten 2-1 at Anfield after a 1-1 draw away.
3. Ipswich Town were beaten 3-2 at Anfield after a 0-0 draw away.
4. Aston Villa.
5. Portsmouth who were beaten on penalties in the replay after both matches ended in a draw.
6. Sunderland.
7. 2-0.
8. Michael Thomas.
9. Ian Rush.
10. Mark Wright.

Chapter 39: FA Cup 1986 – Answers
(questions on page 39)

1. 5-0.
2. Chelsea.
3. York City were beaten 3-1 at Anfield after a 1-1 draw away.
4. Watford were beaten 2-1 away after a 0-0 draw at Anfield.
5. Southampton.
6. Everton in the first ever Merseyside derby final.
7. 3-1.
8. Ian Rush.
9. Ian Rush who scored six goals in total for Liverpool during the competition.
10. Alan Hansen.

(questions on page 40)

1. Doncaster Rovers were beaten 2-0 away after a 2-2 draw at Anfield.
2. Carlisle United were beaten 2-0 away after a 0-0 draw at Anfield.
3. 2-0.
4. Bristol City.
5. Leicester City (after a replay).
6. Newcastle United.
7. 3-0.
8. Kevin Keegan.
9. Kevin Keegan who scored six goals in total for Liverpool during the competition.
10. Emlyn Hughes.

Chapter 41: Steven Gerrard – Answers

(questions on page 41)

1. He was born in Whiston, Merseyside.
2. 9.
3. 18.
4. 23.
5. 710.
6. 473.
7. 4.
8. LA Galaxy.
9. 114.
10. Rangers.

Chapter 42: Emlyn Hughes – Answers
(questions on page 42)

1. Barrow-in-Furness.
2. He died from a brain tumour aged just 57.
3. Blackpool.
4. £65,000.
5. Crazy Horse.
6. Four.
7. Wolverhampton Wanderers.
8. 62
9. Rotherham United.
10. A Question of Sport.

Chapter 43: Jordan Henderson – Answers
(questions on page 43)

1. Sunderland.
2. 6 feet tall.
3. Sunderland.
4. A reported £16 million.
5. He made his Liverpool debut against his old club Sunderland and he received a mixed reception from the fans.
6. In August 2012, Brendan Rodgers told Henderson he could be signed by Fulham but Henderson rejected the move.
7. The first time he was captain was 29th November 2014. He became permanent captain at the start of the 2015/16 season.
8. 2019/20.
9. Midfield.
10. 14.

Chapter 44: Ian Rush – Answers

(questions on page 44)

1. Wales.
2. Chester City.
3. In April 1980 Liverpool paid a record fee for a teenager of £300,000 for Rush.
4. Rush earned the nickname "The Ghost" for the way he snuck up behind defenders.
5. 5.
6. 346.
7. 1984.
8. Juventus.
9. 73.
10. Chester City.

Chapter 45: Mo Salah Answers
(questions on page 45)

1. Egypt.
2. Roma.
3. £36.9 Million.
4. He scored on his debut against Watford on 12th August 2017.
5. He is a devout Muslim.
6. 32 goals. This is a Premier League record for a 38-game season.
7. 2017/18.
8. 2017/18.
9. 70. This is a club record.
10. Salah has various nicknames but is widely known as The Pharaoh as well as of course The Egyptian King.

Chapter 46: Michael Owen – Answers

(questions on page 46)

1. Chester.
2. Midget Gem.
3. 17. He scored on his debut too becoming the youngest ever scorer in the club's history at 17 years and 143 days.
4. 297.
5. 158.
6. Real Madrid.
7. £8 million.
8. 89.
9. 40.
10. 2001.

Chapter 47: Robbie Fowler – Answers
(questions on page 47)

1. He was born in Toxteth, Liverpool.
2. He was called The Toxteth Terror when he was a youngster, but The Kop christened him "God" and the label stuck.
3. 18. He scored on his debut too.
4. 369.
5. 183.
6. Leeds United.
7. £8 million.
8. 26.
9. 7.
10. His first managerial job was at Muangthong United, in Thailand.

1. Bootle.
2. Everton.
3. 6 feet 1 inch tall.
4. He made his debut aged 18, just three weeks before his 19th birthday.
5. 737.
6. 508.
7. 28.
8. 11.
9. Sky Sports.
10. Carra.

Chapter 49: Virgil van Dijk - Answers
(questions on page 49)

1. He was born in Breda in The Netherlands.
2. Southampton.
3. £75 million.
4. Centre half.
5. He scored on his debut against Everton becoming the first player since 1901 to score on debut in the Merseyside Derby.
6. The Dyke.
7. He chooses to use his first name Virgil on his kit because of a feud with his father.
8. Celtic.
9. 2018-19.
10. 2018-19.

Chapter 50: More Nationalities - Answers
(questions on page 50)

1. Lucas Leiva was born in Brazil.
2. Jerzy Dudek was born in Poland.
3. Philippe Coutinho was born in Brazil.
4. Martin Skrtel was born in Slovakia.
5. Javier Mascherano was born in Argentina.
6. Alan Hansen was born in Scotland.
7. Luis Suarez was born in Uruguay.
8. Georginio Wijnaldum was born in the Netherlands.
9. Dietmar Hamann was born in Germany.
10. Sadio Mane was born in Senegal.

Chapter 51: More Shirt Numbers – Answers
(questions on page 51)

1. Dalglish – 7.
2. Hughes – 6.
3. Salah – 10.
4. Rush – 9.
5. Van Dijk – 4.
6. Gerrard – 8.
7. Keegan – 7.
8. Carragher – 23.
9. Souness – 11.
10. Fowler – 9.

Chapter 52: 1960s Transfers - Answers

(questions on page 52)

1. Motherwell.
2. Dundee United.
3. Preston North End.
4. Scunthorpe United.
5. Chelsea.
6. Coventry City.
7. Wolves.
8. Bury.
9. Bristol Rovers.
10. Bolton Wanderers.

(questions on page 53)

1. Cardiff City.
2. Tranmere Rovers.
3. Jimmy Case.
4. Newcastle United.
5. Arsenal.
6. Nottingham Forest.
7. Wrexham.
8. Newcastle United.
9. Home Farm.
10. Vancouver Whitecaps.

Chapter 54: 1980s Transfers – Answers
(questions on page 54)

1. Ayr United.
2. £900,000 which was a club record transfer at the time.
3. Craig Johnston.
4. Everton.
5. Jim Beglin.
6. Ajax.
7. Ipswich Town.
8. Steve McMahon.
9. Sammy Lee.
10. Oxford United.

(questions on page 55)

1. Bournemouth.
2. Derby County.
3. Michael Thomas.
4. Watford.
5. Nottingham Forest.
6. Neil Ruddock.
7. Borussia Dortmund.
8. Crewe Alexandra.
9. £8 million.
10. Lens.

Chapter 56: 2000-2009 Transfers – Answers
(questions on page 56)

1. **1.** Leicester City.
2. **2.** Coventry City.
3. **3.** Feyenoord.
4. **4.** Monaco.
5. **5.** Leeds United.
6. **6.** Real Sociedad.
7. **7.** Luis Garcia.
8. **8.** Villareal.
9. **9.** Feyenoord.
10. **10.** Zenit St Petersburg.

Chapter 57: 2010-2020 Transfers – Answers
(questions on page 57)

1. Newcastle United.
2. Ajax.
3. Chelsea.
4. Inter Milan.
5. Southampton.
6. 1899 Hoffenheim.
7. Manchester City.
8. Southampton.
9. Arsenal.
10. Roma.

Chapter 58: Who Said That? – Answers
(questions on page 58)

1. Bill Shankly.
2. Robbie Fowler.
3. Kevin Keegan.
4. Bob Paisley.
5. Bill Shankly.
6. Bob Paisley.
7. Bruce Grobbelaar.
8. Michael Owen.
9. Bill Shankly.
10. Gerard Houllier.

Chapter 59: Who Said That Too? - Answers
(questions on page 59)

1. Bill Shankly.
2. Luis Suarez.
3. Bill Shankly.
4. Brendan Rodgers.
5. Bill Shankly.
6. Barry Venison.
7. Bill Shankly.
8. Jan Molby.
9. Ian Rush (describing playing in Italy).
10. Bill Shankly.

1. Glasgow.
2. Celtic.
3. 1977.
4. £440,000, which was a British record transfer fee at the time.
5. 1985.
6. 172 goals including 118 in the League.
7. 3.
8. 8.
9. 102. He is the only man to have won more than 100 caps for Scotland.
10. 2018.

Chapter 61: The Final Question
(answer on page 122)

601. What is inscribed on the base of Shankly's statue outside the Kop?
   a) He made the people happy
   b) He made the people smile
   c) He made the people weep

Chapter 62: The Final Answer

(question on page 121)

The statue bears the words, "He made the people happy"

Helping One Another

If you have got some enjoyment from this book, would you please leave a helpful review of it on Amazon. All reviews are very much appreciated.

Also, if you have any comments, or ideas for improvements to this book, you can contact me at conan@johnandcel.co.uk and I do read every email.

Many thanks in advance

Kopite Conan.

Printed in Great Britain
by Amazon